FRANCIS FRITH'S
TOWN & CITY
MEMORIES

HULL

GRAHAM WILKINSON was born into a large fishing family and has lived in Hull all his life. A local historian, he is the author and co-author of several local history books and is well known for his interest and research into the social and living conditions of the 19th century.

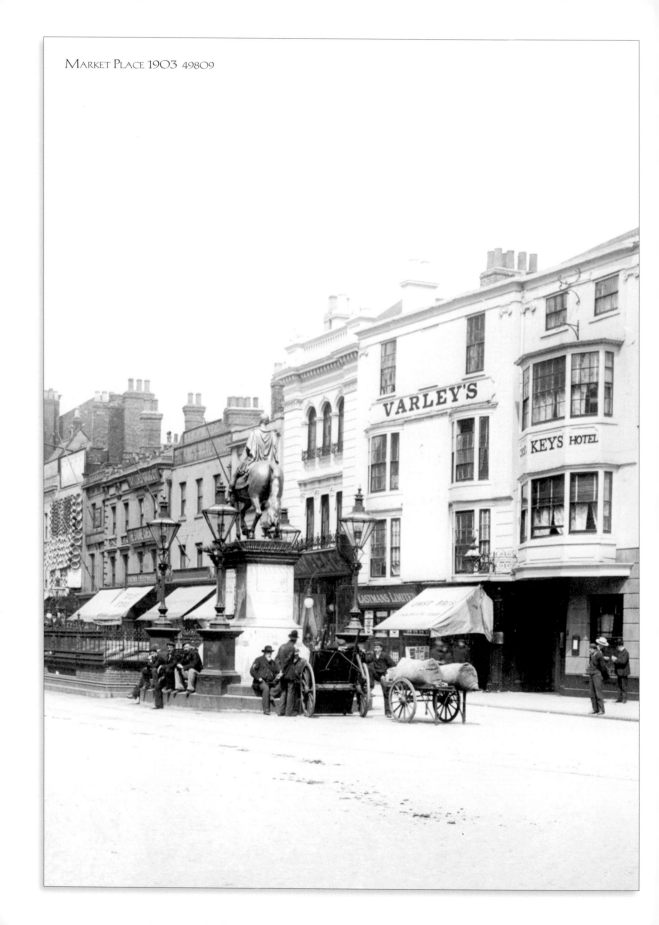

FRANCIS FRITH'S

TOWN & CITY

MEMORIES

HULL

GRAHAM WILKINSON

FRANCIS FRITH'S
TOWN & CITY
MEMORIES

First published as Hull, A Photographic History of your Town
in 2001 by Black Horse Books, an imprint of The Francis Frith Collection
Revised edition published in the United Kingdom in 2006 by
The Francis Frith Collection as Hull, Town and City Memories
Limited Hardback Edition ISBN 1-84589-134-1
Paperback Edition ISBN 1-84589-135-X

British Library Cataloguing in Publication Data

Hull
Town and City Memories
Graham Wilkinson

The Francis Frith Collection®
Frith's Barn, Teffont,
Salisbury, Wiltshire SP3 5QP
Tel: +44 (0) 1722 716 376
Email: info@francisfrith.co.uk
www.francisfrith.com

Aerial photographs reproduced under licence from Simmons Aerofilms Limited
Historical Ordnance Survey maps reproduced under licence from Homecheck.co.uk

Printed and bound in England

Front Cover: **HULL, MARKET PLACE 1903** 49809t
The colour-tinting in this image is for illustrative purposes only,
and is not intended to be historically accurate

FRANCIS FRITH'S

TOWN&CITY

MEMORIES

CONTENTS

THE MAKING OF AN ARCHIVE

Francis Frith, Victorian founder of the world-famous photographic archive, was a devout Quaker and a highly successful Victorian businessman. By 1860 he was already a multi-millionaire, having established and sold a wholesale grocery business in Liverpool. He had also made a series of pioneering photographic journeys to the Nile region. The images he returned with were the talk of London. An eminent modern historian has likened their impact on the population of the time to that on our own generation of the first photographs taken on the surface of the moon.

Frith had a passion for landscape, and was as equally inspired by the countryside of Britain as he was by the desert regions of the Nile. He resolved to set out on a new career and to use his skills with a camera. He established a business in Reigate as a specialist publisher of topographical photographs.

Frith lived in an era of immense and sometimes violent change. For the poor in the early part of Victoria's reign work was a drudge and the hours long, and ordinary people had precious little free time. Most had not travelled far beyond the boundaries of their own town or village. Mass tourism was in its infancy during the 1860s, but during the next decade the railway network and the establishment of Bank Holidays and half-Saturdays gradually made it possible for the working man and his family to enjoy holidays and to see a little more of the world. With characteristic business acumen, Francis Frith foresaw that these new tourists would enjoy having souvenirs to commemorate their days out. He began selling photo-souvenirs of seaside resorts and beauty spots, which the Victorian public pasted into treasured family albums.

Frith's aim was to photograph every town and village in Britain. For the next thirty years he travelled the country by train and by pony and trap, producing fine photographs of seaside resorts and beauty spots that were keenly bought by millions of Victorians.

THE RISE OF FRITH & CO

Each photograph was taken with tourism in mind, the small team of Frith photographers concentrating on busy shopping streets, beaches, seafronts, picturesque lanes and villages. They also photographed buildings: the Victorian and Edwardian eras were times of huge building activity, and town halls, libraries, post offices, schools and technical colleges were springing up all over the country. They were invariably celebrated by a proud Victorian public, and photo souvenirs – visual records – published by F Frith & Co were sold in their hundreds of thousands. In addition, many new commercial buildings such as hotels, inns and pubs were photographed, often because their owners specifically commissioned Frith postcards or prints of them for re-sale or for publicity purposes.

In order to gain some understanding of the scale of Frith's business one only has to look at the catalogue issued by Frith & Co in 1886: it runs to some 670 pages. By 1890 Frith had created the greatest specialist photographic publishing company in the world, with over 2,000 stockists! The picture on the right shows the Frith & Co display board on the wall of the stockist at Ingleton in the Yorkshire Dales (left of window). Beautifully constructed with a mahogany frame and gilt inserts, it displayed a dozen scenes.

The Making of an Archive

Postcard Bonanza

The ever-popular holiday postcard we know today took many years to appear, and F Frith & Co was in the vanguard of its development. Postcards became a hugely popular means of communication and sold in their millions. Frith's company took full advantage of this boom and soon became the major publisher of photographic view postcards.

Francis Frith died in 1898 at his villa in Cannes, his great project still growing. His sons Eustace and Cyril continued their father's monumental task, expanding the number of views offered to the public and recording more and more places in Britain, as the coasts and countryside were opened up to mass travel. The archive Frith created continued in business for another seventy years. By 1970 it contained over a third of a million pictures of 7,000 cities, towns and villages. The massive photographic record Frith has left to us stands as a living monument to a special and very remarkable man.

This book shows Hull as it was photographed by this world-famous archive at various periods in its development over the past 150 years. Every photograph was taken for a specific commercial purpose, which explains why the selection may not show every aspect of the town landscape. However, the photographs, compiled from one of the world's most celebrated archives, provide an important and absorbing record of your town.

FROM THE AIR

HULL FROM THE AIR 1925 AF12693

INTRODUCTION

HULL, or more correctly Kingston-upon-Hull, is situated on the north side of the River Humber at a point where the River Hull empties the waters drained from the Holderness Plain of the East Riding of Yorkshire.

The town began its life in the 12th century, as a hamlet named Wyke upon Hull, which was then in the possession of the monks of nearby Meaux Abbey who had developed a small port for their wool trade. Noticed by King Edward I as an ideal location for a supply base for his campaign against the Scots, the town was acquired by him in 1293 and subsequently re-named Kingstown-upon-Hull. Enjoying royal patronage, it received its first charter in 1299; after this, the town began to flourish, and soon became one of the foremost ports of the realm, being only surpassed in trade by Liverpool and London.

The town was fortified during the 14th century when massive brick walls with many towers were constructed to protect the inhabitants; five principal gates gave entry and exit across the moat to the town. The city was viewed as a prize during the Wars of the Roses, but stayed loyal to the house of Lancaster. Its military importance was recognised again when the town was further fortified during the 16th century. King Henry VIII ordered a huge castle to be constructed, but this time on the east bank of the River Hull. The castle, or 'The Citadel' as it was known, was built to a high specification with many bastions, blockhouses and turrets. Sad to say, none of the town walls or castle fortifications remain to their original height for the visitor to see; they were removed for the expansion of the town during the 18th and 19th centuries.

INTRODUCTION

INTRODUCTION

The town was again regarded as a strategic prize by the Royalists and Parliamentarians during the English Civil War. Local historians will tell you that the war started in Hull: on 23 April 1642, King Charles I was refused entry at the north-west gate, then known as the Beverley Gate, so setting in motion a chain of events that was eventually to lead to his death. A section of the town walls was excavated a few years ago; the massive brick foundations were found to be in a wonderful state of preservation. The walls have been preserved in situ, and a viewing area has been constructed around them at the west end of the Whitefriargate.

Following the construction of Hull's first dock in 1778, then the largest inland dock in the kingdom, trade and the city grew rapidly. So successful was the port that several more docks were to follow during the 19th century, eventually resulting in the city being completely ringed by water. The railway came to the city in 1840 with the building of the Hull & Selby Railway. This added to the prosperity of the town, and in turn led to the construction of several more docks to the east and west of the city to cope with the increase in trade.

The first quarter of the 19th century saw Hull become the biggest whaling port in Britain, processing whale oil, seal skins, whale-bone and other attendant products. As the whale fishery came to an end during the 1860s, the city moved forward and became the world's largest centre for oil seed crushing and milling; this led to the establishment of many industries such as paint, colour, oil and varnish manufacture. Joseph Rank the miller began his working life in Hull during the 19th century, and became the largest flour miller in the country.

The port was once the home of the world's largest deepwater fishing fleet, and it is often said that the kipper was invented in Hull. The largest part of the city's trade was conducted with the Scandinavian countries, the Baltic states and the low countries of Europe; wool, coal, iron, machinery and grain were major exports, and

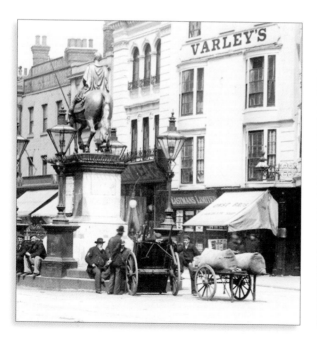 

DETAILS FROM 49809, 49807, 49820 AND 49823

large quantities of timber, oil seed, fruit and provisions accounted for the import trade. During the late 19th and early 20th century, the port was home to the merchant ships of the Wilson Line; at the beginning of the 20th century, this was the world's largest privately-owned mercantile fleet, owning just short of 100 steamships.

The town was the home and birthplace of several famous names in English history. They include the De La Pole family, the richest merchants in the kingdom during the reign of Edward III; the great poet and patriot Andrew Marvell, born in March 1621 in the nearby village of Winestead, MP for Hull for 20 years, a friend of John Milton and admirer of Oliver Cromwell; Joseph Rank, the pioneer of modern milling and one of the town's greatest benefactors; and William Wilberforce, the great emancipator and abolitionist.

The city was one of the few towns or cities that suffered badly during both world wars - it was bombed on both occasions. During the Second World War the city was the most bombed centre of occupation after London, sustaining 82 air raids with 1200 killed and over 3,000 injured. Out of a housing stock of 92,660, only 5,945 houses remained unscathed, and most of the grand buildings which once adorned the main thoroughfares of the city centre were either obliterated or seriously damaged. The large-scale clearances which followed the Second World War resulted in large parts of the city being rebuilt during the 1950s. The city centre has undergone large-scale changes and modernisation, and its town centre docks have been redeveloped and no longer cater for any mercantile trade. The former Queens Dock was filled during the 1930s, and is now the town's municipal Queen's Gardens; the Humber Dock and Railway Dock have been converted into a thriving marina; and the Princes Dock, whilst still containing a large expanse of water, is now one of the principal shopping areas following redevelopment during the 1980s and early 1990s.

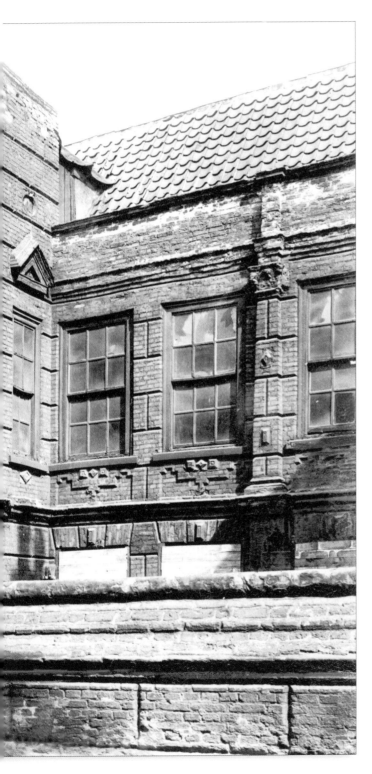

WILBERFORCE HOUSE 1903 49835

This house, according to tradition, was owned and built during the 16th century by the Lister family, who entertained King Charles I here in 1639. The house was extensively added to and re-modelled along the years, and contains many architectural features from the 16th to the 20th century. During the 18th century the house was the home of the wealthy Wilberforce family. It was here in 1759 that the great emancipator William Wilberforce was born. The family were merchants and corn dealers, and had their own staithe (landing stage) adjoining the house. The building evolved and changed hands throughout the years, eventually becoming offices and business premises for several of the city's corn and seed merchants.

THE WILBERFORCE MUSEUM c1955 H133019

Following its purchase and closure during the early 1900s by the city council, the house was completely refurbished. It re-opened during 1906 as the Wilberforce House museum, and is now the home of an extensive collection of artefacts relating to the slave trade; the abolition of the slave trade was to take up most of William's political life. He died in 1833, and is buried in Westminster Abbey.

THE OLD TOWN & THE MARKET PLACE

MUCH of the property in Hull's Old Town and Market Place had evolved over several hundred years; it was a mixture of large riverside warehouses, commercial properties, small businesses and scattered areas of housing. The town's situation on the east side of the country meant that most of its trade was conducted with the Scandinavian countries, the Baltic States, the Hanseatic ports and the low countries of Europe. The centre of Hull's merchant trade was conducted in the High Street alongside the 'Old Harbour' (the name given to the lower reaches of the River Hull where it entered the River Humber). The High Street, formerly known as Hull Street, followed the sinuous line of the river; the merchants built many substantial and richly-adorned houses along its frontage adjoining their staithes (private wharves). The names of the merchants who built these houses or were associated with them are reflected in the superb examples that survive today: Blaydes House, the Maister House, Crowle House and the superb Wilberforce House (see 49835 and H133019, pages 14-15).

Several Hull merchants became very wealthy and influential. One family in particular, the De La Poles, progressed from their beginnings as humble merchants to aldermen and mayors of the town; they eventually rose to become the richest merchant family in the land, and were created Earls of Suffolk under Richard II. The family built a huge mansion named the Suffolk Palace opposite St Mary's Church, Lowgate, on a site once occupied by the city's General Post Office. It is now a large public house belonging to the J D Wetherspoon chain.

MARKET PLACE 1903 49809

The Market Place was for centuries the main area for the town's retail business. It was lined on both sides by every conceivable type of trade or calling including many taverns and inns, with names such as the Reindeer, the Fleece Inn and the Blue Bell. The predominantly 19th-century frontages of the Market Place hide the much older buildings contained within, a fact only discovered when large-scale demolition took place along the east side during the 1970s.

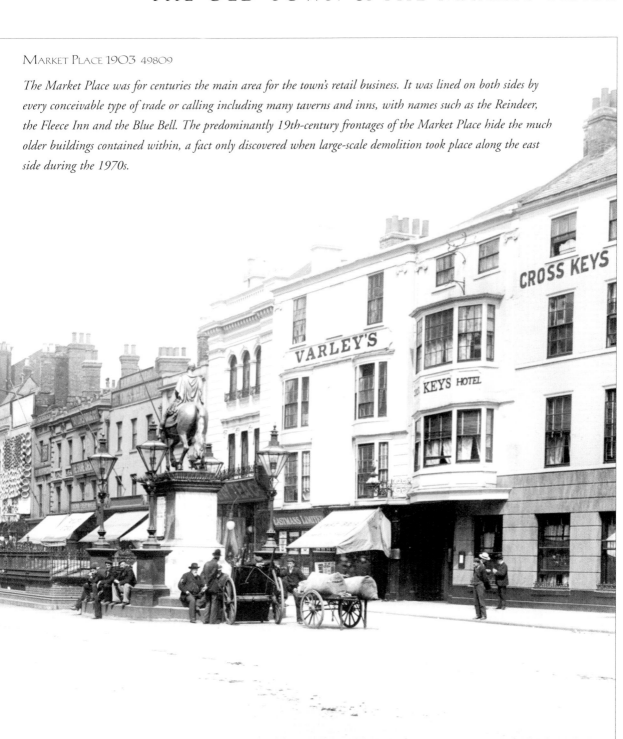

THE OLD TOWN & THE MARKET PLACE

The Lowgate and Marketgate were where the weekly markets have been held in Hull since the last quarter of the 13th century, when a Tuesday and Friday market became established. Although smaller specialised markets were held in various parts of the city, the main market was always held in the Marketgate or Market Place, a site it occupied until the early years of the 20th century.

When Daniel Defoe, in his great work 'A Tour Through The Whole Island of Great Britain', visited the city in the 1720s, he described the city thus: 'The town is exceedingly close built, and should a fire ever be its fate, it might suffer deeply on that account.' Firemen's ladders were kept in a prominent position well into the 20th century - we can see one in 49809, pages 16-17, in the centre of the road beyond the statue.

The Cross Keys Hotel, on the east side of the Market Place (see 49809, pages 16-17), under the stewardship of the Varley family, had been at one time the most important coaching inn in the town, and just as important to Hull as the Savoy was to London. The hotel takes its name from the Archbishops of York, who had a hostelry in this area during the 14th century; their coat of arms consisted of two crossed keys, the sign of St Peter. The building had been an important coaching inn since the 18th century. It had 40 bedrooms and 15 sitting rooms, some of which were named after great national heroes, such as the Wellington room, the Nelson room and the Raleigh room. Trade declined in the late 19th century owing to the speed, regularity and comfort of railway travel. The Cross Keys closed as a hotel in 1922; by 1937 the building

THE KING WILLIAM STATUE C1955 H133006

Two ancient churches occupy sites in the Old Town: St Mary's in nearby Lowgate, and the Church of the Holy Trinity, shown here with its attendant market stalls. The church stands on the site of an earlier chapel, and was consecrated in around 1425. The fabric contains large areas of the earliest surviving medieval brickwork in England, and it is reputedly the largest parish church, by area, in the country.

HOLY TRINITY CHURCH
C1960 H133101

The Old Corn Exchange public house, named from its close proximity to the corn market held nearby since the 1600s, can be seen peering out from behind the north-east corner of the church (right). Beginning life as the Excise Coffee House, the pub changed its name to the Corn Market during the early 1800s before becoming the Old Corn Exchange. Although a new Corn Exchange was erected in the nearby High Street in 1856, the pub retained its old connection and is still trading to this day.

THE OLD TOWN & THE MARKET PLACE

MARKET PLACE 1903 49813

The west side of the Market Place still contains several of its old buildings, including the King William Hotel at No 41, named from its close proximity to the statue; local folk lore says that when the king hears the clock of the nearby Holy Trinity Church strikes midnight, he dismounts and avails himself of a drink in the nearby public house.

had become almost derelict. Just prior to its demolition, it was described in the local paper, the 'Hull Daily Mail', as being 'a large and impressive four-storied building with a double front and stabling for 40 horses. To the rear is a great courtyard in which hangs a bell dated 1596, along with great branches of decorated ironwork from which the oil lamps swung when the steaming horses clattered in on a winter's night'.

The statue to King William III (H133006, page 18)

by the Flemish sculptor Peter Scheemakers, based on the famous equestrian statute of Marcus Aurelius in Rome, is known locally as 'King Billy'. It was erected by public subscription in 1734, for £893 10s, on the site of the town's former bullring; it has stood undisturbed for over 250 years, except when it was removed temporarily for safety during the Second World War. The underground gents' public lavatories were excavated alongside and underneath the statue around the turn of the 20th

THE TOWN HALL 1903 49805

THE GUILDHALL c1955 H133014

century, and have won many awards for their cleanliness and state of preservation. Due to their position in the middle of a major thoroughfare the toilets are now sadly closed but can be viewed by appointment.

This area of the town suffered heavily in the Zeppelin air raids of 1915 when the Edwin Davis & Company store, on the corner of South Church Side (49813, centre right, pages 20-21), was completely obliterated after sustaining a direct hit. The store had occupied the site since 1790, and was probably the only shop in the country to be bombed in two world wars when its new premises to the north of the city centre suffered the same fate in 1941.

Like most large towns, Hull had its Guildhall. It originally occupied a site at the south end of the Market Place not far from Holy Trinity Church, but it had fallen into dereliction by the early 1800s. After occupying various buildings, including Alderman William Jarrett's house, which had been used by the corporation as a temporary Guildhall for a number of years, a new foundation stone was laid in 1862; four years later the new Guildhall was completed (see 49805) on a site to the north of the Market Place, fronting Lowgate between Leadenhall Square and Hanover Square.

The building was designed by Cuthbert Broderick in the Italianate or Classical style, and was sumptuously decorated both internally and externally. This Guildhall survived until 1912, when it was demolished having outgrown its use. Large sections of the building and parts of the tower found a new home in Brantingham, a village to the west of Hull, where a war memorial was constructed from fragments of the fabric; remaining parts of the tower were placed in the city's Pearson Park as architectural features. Chosen by competition, a new Guildhall (H133014) to Renaissance designs by Russell, Cooper and Davis was erected in stages on the same site as the earlier one between 1903 and 1916.

The early years of the 20th century were also a time for great changes in the city: large areas of slum property were swept away, creating wide thoroughfares and large open spaces. But many narrow streets remained in the area once encompassed by the city walls, and still do in various parts of the Old Town.

Whitefriargate (see 49817, pages 26-27), and its eastern extensions of Silver Street and Scale Lane, is part of an ancient street named Aldgate leading from the Beverley Gate deep into the heart of the Old Town. The name Whitefriargate is derived from the road's position alongside the site of a friary belonging to the Carmelites, or White Friars. There was also a Blackfriargate named after the Dominican order of monks, who also had a religious foundation near to the Market Place.

The west end of Whitefriargate was the site of the town's Beverley Gate; it was here that King Charles I was refused admission in 1642. A ceremonial gate or arch was often reconstructed at the west end of the street when subsequent monarchs or members of the Royal family visited the city, perhaps as a token of penance for the townspeople having refused the King entry all those years ago.

Whitefriargate was also the home to several of the major clearing banks, including branches of the Bank of England and the Midland Bank; large national companies such as Marks and Spencer, F W Woolworth and Burton the tailors (H133304, pages 24-25, left) all had major stores here, interspersed with many small businesses such as bakers and confectioners, hairdressers, tobacconists and tea and coffee houses, all contributing to make the area a popular venue for shoppers.

Large-scale redevelopment has taken place in the area, especially along the north side of the street. It is now fully pedestrianised, but the street retains many of its late 18th- and early 19th-century buildings, and above the modern shop fronts the original fine architectural building lines show the modern visitor a glimpse of the street's former grandeur.

WHITEFRIARGATE c1955 H133304

THE OLD TOWN & THE MARKET PLACE

Always a popular business area lined with many fine shops, hotels and taverns, Whitefriargate in the Old Town has remained busy for hundreds of years, and remains so to this day. At the turn of the 20th century, the north side of the street had no fewer than six drinking establishments in the space of a few hundred yards, including the Andrew Marvell, named after Hull's great patriot and poet, the Monument Tavern with its miniature column and statue of William Wilberforce the emancipator and abolitionist, the Burns Head, the Red Lion, the Flower Pot and the grand George Hotel coaching inn, none of which survive.

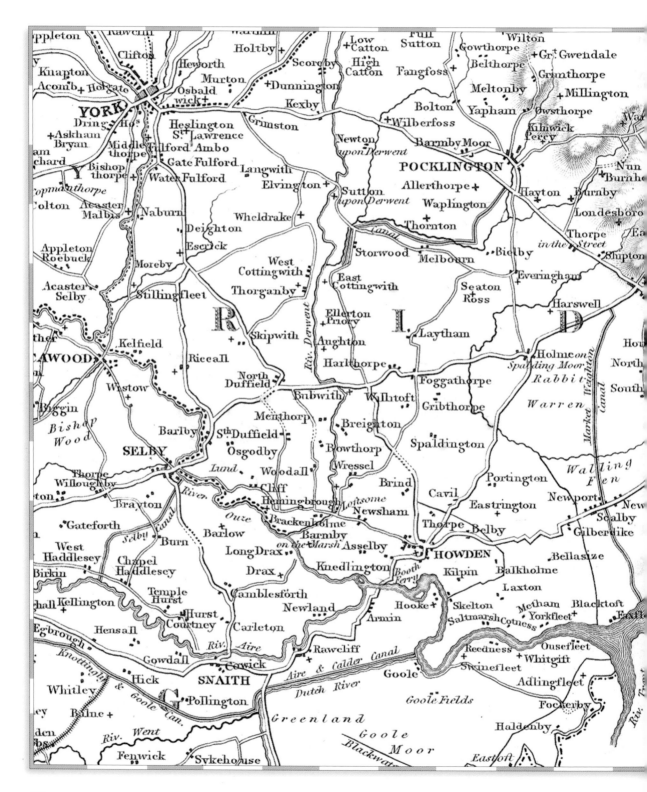

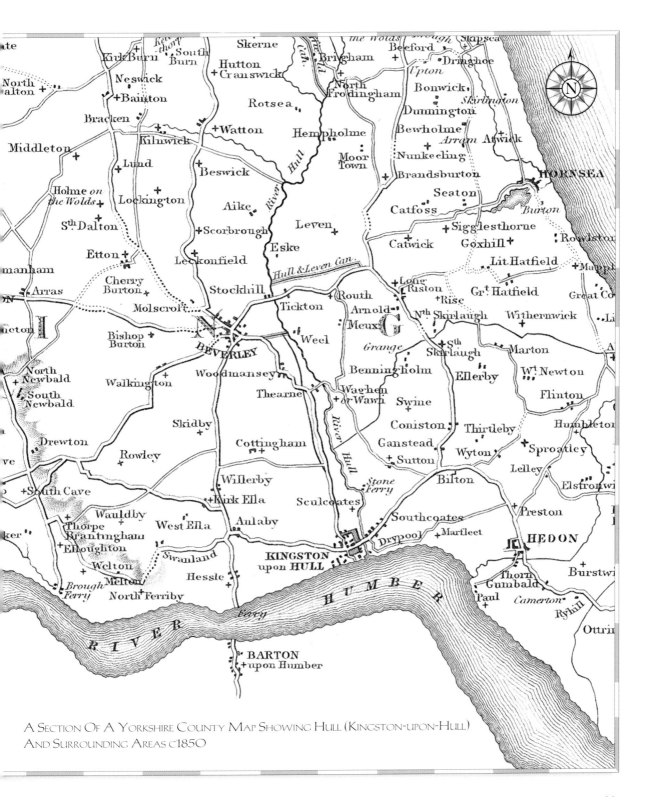

A SECTION OF A YORKSHIRE COUNTY MAP SHOWING HULL (KINGSTON-UPON-HULL)
AND SURROUNDING AREAS c1850

GEORGIAN, VICTORIAN & EDWARDIAN SUBURBS

GEORGE STREET 1903 49814

*The corner opposite the Hull Savings Bank was
also redeveloped around 1884 as a retail wine
and spirit vaults belonging to Henry Wilson,
wine and spirit merchant (right); the vaults
adjoined his large offices, which were known
as Savile House. The public house, built in
gin palace style, and the grand offices were
known thereafter as Wilson's Corner. Although
the offices have disappeared, the public house
remains unaltered; although officially called the
Dram Shop, the pub is still known locally as
Wilson's Corner. The electric tram approaching
the statute of Hull's famous poet Andrew
Marvell is returning to the city centre; it carries
an 'H' route letter, denoting the Holderness
Road. Several theatres occupied sites on George
Street, including the Grand Theatre, the
Princes Hall and the Empire Music Hall.*

Georgian, Victorian & Edwardian Suburbs

George Street c1960 H133073

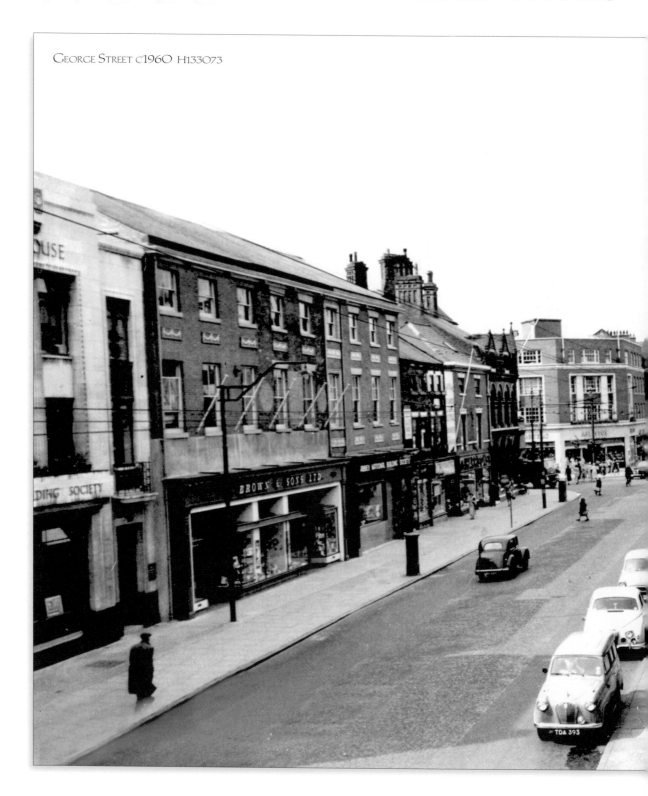

Georgian, Victorian & Edwardian Suburbs

FOLLOWING the demolition of the northern town walls and the construction of the first dock in 1778, the town could now spread north and west. The spoil from the excavations was deposited on the Dock Estate Company's land, which slightly raised the surrounding area. George Street (49814, pages 30-31) was developed by the Hull Dock Company, and was the town's first Georgian suburb. Although the town lies below sea level, the raising of this area allowed for some grand buildings to be erected, many with sub-basements and cellars.

The Hull Savings Bank was established in 1818. It occupied various sites throughout the town before becoming established in Posterngate, where it remained for over 50 years. The expansion and growth of banking reflected Hull's rise as a trading centre, and the Hull Savings Bank moved to new premises at the junction of George Street and Smeaton Street in 1884 (49814, left), built to the designs of Robert Clamp. The bank was unusual in that it had its own elementary school between 1831-1851, the only known example anywhere in the country.

Although once containing some fine residential property, George Street soon became taken over by the business community, including several banks, building societies and Hull's very own Selfridges - the famous Carmichael's department store. George Street suffered damage during the Second World War, and the area has changed with the times as various businesses have come and gone. But the aforementioned Wilson's Corner and the family book store of Brown & Sons (see H133073, left) are all features of George Street which have remained as familiar landmarks to the townspeople.

Hull was the birthplace of the great emancipator William Wilberforce (1759-1833). At the age of 21 he was elected MP for Hull; he is mainly remembered for his campaign to abolish slavery. Following his death in 1833, he was buried in Westminster Abbey; a tall fluted Doric column (see 49807, right), 90ft high and surmounted by a 12ft statue, was erected to his memory a year later - the first stone was laid on 1 August 1834, the date of the abolition of slavery in the British Colonies.

GEORGIAN, VICTORIAN & EDWARDIAN SUBURBS

The demolition of large areas of slum property outside the former city walls at the turn of the 20th century led to wide thoroughfares and open squares ripe for development. One such area was King Edward Street, which was cleared during the early 1900s to become the focal point for a new city centre and town square. It was surrounded by fine buildings such as the magnificent and newly-opened Prudential Insurance building with its circular tower (49810, page 38), designed by Alfred Waterhouse & Son.

The opening out of the part of the town outside the former city walls also enabled the new electric tram system to operate into the heart of the city and business district. The new square near King Edward Street (49810, pages 38-39) became a junction for all the city routes. Sad to say, this area of the town centre was totally obliterated during the night of 7 May 1941 when it sustained massive damage during the wartime air raids. King Edward Street was completely obliterated along with Waterworks Street, and 15 people who were sheltering in the basement of the Prudential Tower tragically lost their lives.

THE DOCK OFFICES 1903 49807

Less than 100 years after the construction of the first dock, the trade of the port was such that Hull required its third major upgrade of its dock offices. The magnificent Grade II listed building in the Venetian Renaissance style was designed by Christopher G Wray and built between 1867 and 1871. The triangular-shaped building with its distinctive three domes was acquired by the city council in 1968 and converted into the Town Docks Museum, the home of Hull's maritime history.

GEORGIAN, VICTORIAN & EDWARDIAN SUBURBS

The statue of Queen Victoria escaped serious damage during the blitz, but the nearby City Hall, by city architect J H Hirst and constructed between 1903-1909 in the Renaissance style, was severely damaged and did not open again until 1950. The site of the blitzed Prudential Insurance buildings became the new Queens House development in 1951.

Waterworks Street was an old street that took its name from its close proximity to the town's first waterworks, which were situated in this area in the 17th century. Following its destruction in the Second World War, it became the eastern extension of Paragon Street (H133068, page 44), when the destroyed and badly damaged 19th-century buildings were swept away to build a unified city centre.

THE DOCK OFFICES 1903 49806

The Wilberforce Memorial, costing £1,250 and funded by public subscription, occupied a site opposite the Dock Offices (left) near to the bridge over the lock gates connecting Princes Dock and Queen's Dock. The bridge was henceforth known as Monument Bridge. Owing to traffic problems encountered following large-scale improvements to the area, the column was moved to a site at the east end of the town's Queens Gardens in 1935.

King Edward Street 1903 49810

GEORGIAN, VICTORIAN & EDWARDIAN SUBURBS

Left: THE QUEEN VICTORIA STATUE c1955 H133011

The 35ft statue of Queen Victoria, designed by the architect J S Gibson and the sculptor H C Fehr, dominated the centre of the new city square following its unveiling by the Prince of Wales on 12 May 1903. The new square soon became known as Queen Victoria Square. After standing alone for a number of years, the statue was raised into the air to accommodate new subterranean municipal lavatories.

Bottom Left: KING EDWARD STREET c1960 H133067

The wide thoroughfares created during the late Victorian period allowed for easy reconstruction; streets such as King Edward Street, cut through in 1901, soon became lined once again with fine shops after the war, such as Hepworth's the tailors and Boots the Chemists.

Below: QUEEN VICTORIA SQUARE c1955 H133013

Georgian, Victorian & Edwardian Suburbs

Paragon Street 1903 49815

Although lined with taverns and ale houses, Paragon Street had its White House Hotel (left), an oasis of temperance amongst its neighbours; the building was a tea and coffee house belonging to the Hull People's Public House Company, and was one of 18 in the city which provided a decent lunch and a non-alcoholic drink for the working man. Being surrounded on all sides by its competitors, the White House became licensed during the 1920s; it is now the large and imposing Yates Wine Lodge.

The west end of Paragon Street took its name from the late 18th-century inn of the same name, which occupied the corner of the nearby Chariot Street. The street was laid out around 1802, and soon many taverns, hotels, inns and shops were built. The famous New Amphitheatre was built in 1846 at the junction with South Street: with its Paragon Street frontage of 206ft in length, and seating approximately 3,000 people, it was at one time one of the largest theatres in the country. Following many name changes, it was partially demolished after becoming unsafe. In 1871 the grand Italianate structure known as the Imperial Hotel was built on the site of its auditorium. Remodelled and rebuilt, the theatre opened as a smaller venue named the Theatre Royal until 1909, when it too closed (see 49815, right); it re-opened as the Tivoli Theatre in 1912.

GEORGIAN, VICTORIAN & EDWARDIAN SUBURBS

PARAGON STREET C1960 H133068

The city of Hull is unique in having its own municipally-owned telephone company, Kingston Communications Ltd, and its distinctive yellow painted boxes were once a common sight all over the city; we can see one just to the left of centre.

Arthur Lucan, of 'Old Mother Riley' fame, tragically died in the theatre on 17 May 1954 just before going on stage for a performance of 'Old Mother Riley in Paris'; he is buried in the city's Eastern Cemetery.

Although extensively redeveloped, Paragon Street retains several of its older buildings, and also a magnificent

late 19th-century grade II listed Gothic Revival glass-roofed arcade designed by Sir Alfred Gelder.

Adjacent to and parallel with Paragon Street ran Carr Lane (49816, pages 46-47), the main route out of the city to the west. Carr is a later corruption of the Norse word 'kjarr' meaning 'wet, boggy marshlands'; the area

Georgian, Victorian & Edwardian Suburbs

immediately to the west of the city was indeed always wet, marshy and prone to flooding. Being the main route to the west, Carr Lane contained its usual quota of 18th-century coaching inns and taverns. Two of them are worthy of note: the Black Horse, sadly lost in the blitz, and the White Horse immediately opposite, demolished and rebuilt during the 1950s but still occupying its original site.

The buildings fronting the north side of Carr Lane were demolished and cleared for the erection of the new City Hall, which opened in 1909.

Sir William Alfred Gelder (1855-1943) was the son of a West Hull village farmer, a self-made man and a successful architect. He was described by

THE NEW POLICE STATION c1903 49833

Grand buildings were eventually to line both sides of Alfred Gelder Street; one of them was a new purpose-built police headquarters, which opened on 25 March 1904. The new building, with its imposing and austere façade, replaced the old central police station that had occupied the site of the former Charity Hall around the corner in nearby Parliament Street. The new building contained 24 cells, and was built in a 'U' shape with offices flanking the corridors. It closed in the 1950s, and the site was sold to the Littlewoods store group for an extension to their department store.

GEORGIAN, VICTORIAN & EDWARDIAN SUBURBS

some historians as doing for Hull what Sir Christopher Wren had done for London. He was Lord Mayor of Hull in five successive years, MP for Brigg, and knighted in 1903. His plans, around the turn of the 20th century, for clearing the town centre of dilapidated slum property by creating wide and airy thoroughfares was to shape the city into the layout which still exists today. The early 1900s saw a new street constructed through a very unsavoury district to link the bridge spanning the town docks with the bridge spanning the river Hull at Drypool. It was named Alfred Gelder Street (see 49833, page 45) in honour of the man who had done so much to reform and re-shape the city.

CARR LANE 1903 49816

Two electric tram routes operated along the length of Carr Lane, route 'A' to the Anlaby Road, and route 'D' along the Hessle Road to the hamlet of Dairycoates at the end of the western extremity of the town borough. Gas had been commercially available in Hull since 1821, and the shop shown on the corner of Chariot Street, G W Smith & Son, carried gas fittings of every description (left). Above the shop we can see a shield bearing the legend 'National Telephone Co No 594': a telephone system had existed in Hull since 1880, and the National Telephone Company was the main rival to the municipal company, which was set up in the city in 1903. By 1910 the local company was making a profit; it is probably still the envy of many cities: for a set monthly charge you can make as many local calls whenever you like, for as often as you like, for as long as you like at no extra cost.

THE WATERFRONT & THE DOCKS

KINGSTON-UPON-HULL had been a major port since its foundation in the 13th century, and the waterfront was always busy. The River Humber, a natural barrier between Yorkshire and Lincolnshire, was a thriving area for the dozens of ferries and steam packets that plied their trade between the two counties. Ferries had existed since the 14th century, and were a vital communication with the capital and the various villages along the estuary. Barton, Barrow, Goxhill, and New Holland all had their own ferries connecting with the town, along with the market boats, which attended the town on market days; travelling between the two banks of the river by ferry would have appeared as commonplace as hopping on a bus today.

THE HUMBER 1903 49820

The ferry boat dock had originally occupied a site inside the entrance to the River Hull, but trade increased to such an extent that by the beginning of the 19th century a purpose-built ferry boat dock was constructed on land reclaimed from the River Humber and part of the old Artillery Ground at the south end. A dock in name only, it took the form of a wooden pier constructed parallel with the River Humber to facilitate landings in rough seas.

THE WATERFRONT & THE DOCKS

THE WATERFRONT & THE DOCKS

Left: THE PIER 1903 49823

Below Left: THE PIER 1903 49821

The Humber Iron Works on the east bank of the River Hull entrance (49823, left) occupied the site of Martin Samuelson's ship yard; in 1863 the yard had built more iron-clad ships than any other yard in the kingdom. So famous was the yard that to this day the site is still known as 'Sammy's Point'. It is now the home of Kingston upon Hull's millennium project, a marine life centre entitled 'The Deep'. One view from the waterfront was to remain part of the scene for over 40 years: in 1868 the old 50-gun HMS 'Southampton' arrived in the river, where she became a sail training ship and boys' reformatory (centre left, 49823).

The Humber foreshore was a popular area for taking in the fresh river air, especially at weekends when the Minerva and Victoria piers were thronged with hundreds of people. No longer catering for river traffic, the pier today is smaller and quieter than it was in its heyday; but it still remains a popular place for a pleasant stroll on a fine day. The River Hull, with its dozens of warehouses and wharves, made a busy highway for the hundreds of large and small craft that earned their living serving the many businesses that lined both banks, and its entrance alongside the Victoria Pier made the pier a popular viewing area.

The Humber keel boats, with their distinctive ketch-rigged sails, and the many paddle steamers were a common sight from the pier. Although primarily used as ferries between the two counties, they were very popular as small cruise boats with the people who could afford the fare. Seven boats a day ran between Hull and Grimsby, several to Barton and New Holland and one a day to Gainsborough, Thorne, Selby, Goole and York. The many paddle steamers, such as the 'Isle of Axholme' and the 'Manchester' (49821, centre), made a very good living at weekends during the summer months offering short cruises along the river at reasonable prices.

The town's success as a port meant that it was continually upgrading its facilities to keep up with trade following the construction of Hull's first dock in 1778. Three more town docks were to follow: Humber Dock in 1809, Junction Dock (later Prince's Dock) in 1829 and the Railway Dock in 1846. The two original docks had been

THE WATERFRONT & THE DOCKS

served by small offices alongside the lock gates, but as trade increased new ones were built at the north end of the High Street in 1820. These new dock offices lasted less than 50 years, and were themselves replaced by the triangular-shaped buildings of 1867-71 (49808).

Although the lock gates and the bridge carrying the road have long since disappeared, this area of the town is still referred to as Monument Bridge, named from the tall column carrying the statue of William Wilberforce.

Prince's Dock (see 49824, page 54) served, amongst others, the UK ports of Aberdeen, Ipswich and Grangemouth, along with the continental ports of Rotterdam, Hamburg and Bremen. As ships became larger, Prince's Dock's trade declined as larger docks were built to the east and west of the city. Its trade relied on the smaller coastal craft and the city's trawler fleet, whose ships were fitted out in the nearby yard of C D Holmes Engineering Co. Following its closure in 1968, Prince's Dock remained derelict for a number of years. However, it still survives following its redevelopment as the Prince's Quay shopping centre, which is built on stilts; the dock retains a large expanse of water and its original walls.

THE DOCK OFFICES AND THE WILBERFORCE MONUMENT 1903 49808

A competition was held to design a new and much larger suite of offices, and the Venetian Renaissance style of C G Wray of London was the winner. It remains one of the city's most popular public buildings in its modern guise as home of the city's whaling and maritime museum.

THE WATERFRONT & THE DOCKS

PRINCE'S DOCK 1903 49824

The foundation stone of Junction Dock was laid in 1827. When it opened in 1829, it formed the last link of a chain of three docks that connected the River Hull with the River Humber, encircling the old town along the line of the former fortifications. The dock was re-named Prince's Dock in 1854 following a visit by Queen Victoria and the Prince Consort.

Following the demolition of the city's fortifications and the construction of the town docks, the city now began a rapid expansion in all directions. More docks were needed to keep pace with the boom in trade, and over the next 100 years the city was to undergo the roller-coaster ride of expansion and contraction of world trade. Outside of the confines of the old town, a new dock, Victoria Dock (see H133044) was planned to run parallel to the River Humber, and this time it was to be on the east shore of the River Hull. Although only served by a single connecting road bridge, the east side of the city was chosen as the site because of its proximity to the River Hull basin, from which access to the new dock was to be gained.

Although most of the trade for the new Victoria Dock came from the Scandinavian and Baltic ports, a large foreign cattle depot with slaughterhouses and chilling facilities was constructed to handle the importation of animals from the Americas. The Victoria Dock closed on 1 February 1970. It is now a rapidly expanding 'dockland village', with hundreds of waterside houses alongside the River Humber.

Following the discovery of the Silver Pits fishing grounds in the North Sea in 1850, the town's fishing industry saw a sudden and massive expansion take place. Space for the mercantile and fishing interests was always a cause of friction in the town, and space had yet again run out. After always playing second fiddle to the mercantile fleet, the fishing industry was now becoming more powerful. A new dock to the west of the town was opened in 1869 (see H133041, page 56): known throughout its construction as the Western Dock, on the day of its opening, 22 July 1869, it was named the Albert Dock after Albert Edward, Prince of Wales, who performed the ceremony. An extension named after the chairman of the Hull Dock Company, William Wright, was added in 1873.

St Andrew's Dock (see H133037, page 56) was originally intended for the use of the coal industry. Immediately upon opening in 1883, it was named after the patron saint of fishermen and handed over for the exclusive use of the town's 420 fishing smacks. The fishing industry expanded and became so successful that by 1895 an extension was commissioned, which duly opened in 1897. By the early years of the 20th century, St Andrew's Dock became home to the world's largest deep-water fishing fleet.

UNLOADING AT VICTORIA DOCK c1955 H133044

The Victoria Dock was opened in 1850, in an area of the town once occupied by the ancient hamlet of Drypool, and rapidly became the home of the town's timber import trade. A happy marriage of a booming export trade in coal also meant that the newly-emptied coal wagons could immediately fill with pit props from the timber yards for their return journey to the West Riding of Yorkshire coalfields.

THE WATERFRONT & THE DOCKS

ALBERT DOCK C1955 H133041

Initially the home of the fishing fleet, the Albert Dock soon became the dock for the importation of wood pulp, paper, fruit and provisions and for the export of heavy vehicles, cars and industrial and agricultural machinery. The dock is still open today; but with the reduction in cargo handling due to containerisation, the Albert Dock has once again become the home of the city's fishing fleet.

ST ANDREW'S DOCK C1955 H133037

St Andrew's Dock was unique in that all the main activities concerned with the upkeep and maintenance of a large fishing fleet took place on and around the dock estate. The dock had the largest ice manufactory in Europe, capable of producing over 1,000 tons a day; the largest fishmeal plant in the world; the busiest postal and telegraph office in the country; and several banks, shops and cafés.

THE WATERFRONT & THE DOCKS

ALEXANDRA DOCK C1955 H133048

From the 1770s, the Hull Dock Company had enjoyed carte blanche regarding shipping facilities in the city; but this was to change during the 1880s with the formation of the Hull, Barnsley and West Riding Junction Railway and Dock Company. A new dock was begun in 1881 on a site to the east of the Victoria Dock; it was almost twice the size of anything built so far. On opening in 1885, it was named after Princess Alexandra, the wife of the Prince of Wales. The dock was the first to be built in Hull for the accommodation of the much larger and newer steam vessels then rapidly taking over from sail.

THE WATERFRONT & THE DOCKS

An economic survey of the 1950s stated that there were probably 50,000 people, or one fifth of the population, involved with the fishing industry. Tragedy and the harsh and terrible working conditions were always a part of the history of the fish dock, and thousands of lives were lost throughout its 92 years, both in fishing and in the defence of the country through two world wars. The double trawler tragedy of 1955, when the 'Lorella' and the 'Roderigo' were lost with the loss of 40 lives; the triple trawler tragedy of 1968 when the 'St Romanus', the 'Kingston Peridot' and the 'Ross Cleveland' sank with the loss of 58 lives; and more recently the 'Gaul', are etched forever in the hearts and minds of the proud fishing community. Sad to say, the dock closed in 1975. Hardly any trace remains of this once vast industry. The site has now been redeveloped as the St Andrew's Quay leisure and retail complex.

Originally intended as another coal dock, the success of Alexandra Dock (49825 and H133048) was guaranteed from the start, as the newer steam vessels were turned around more quickly. As trade increased to all parts of the world, the dock soon became home to all manner of goods and commodities, including large quantities of timber, fruit and vegetables, and grain and oil seeds of every description. Ships with exotic home ports, such as Vera Cruz, Rosario, Pernambuco, Karachi and Havana, were a common sight in the dock following the establishment of the long trade routes to Australia, South America and Asia. The dock closed in 1982, but owing to the increased demand for port facilities it re-opened to shipping in 1991.

King George Dock (H133058), the largest of the town's nine docks, had a total water area of 53 acres and could accommodate the largest ships. The massive coal exports that left the port (having been transported via its connections with over 380 pits in the Yorkshire, Nottinghamshire and Derbyshire coalfields), and the huge imports of grain, were to dominate the dock's trade for many years. With its 23 coaling berths, its 40,000-ton grain silo, its three acres of wool sheds and its tea, fruit, meat and vegetable transit sheds, the dock was a hive of

The Waterfront & the Docks

Left: Alexandra Dock 1903 49825

Below Left: King George Dock c1960 H133058

The last piece of the jigsaw that was to complete the picture of Hull's docks arrived just before the First World War with the opening of the first dock in the country to use electric power throughout. Built jointly by the Hull & Barnsley Railway Company and the North Eastern Railway Company, it was originally to be called the Joint Dock, but it was named King George Dock on its opening on 26 June 1914 by King George V.

Below: The Dock Offices and the Gardens c1955 H133002

Queens Gardens c1955 H133026

The Waterfront & the Docks

activity in all four corners. In 1951, in its role as the travelling section of the Festival of Britain, the aircraft carrier HMS 'Campania' visited the port and attracted thousands of visitors, some of whom queued for hours to view the exhibitions on board. The dock thrives today. It is the English home of the huge P & O North Sea Ferries Company, who use the largest roll-on roll-off ferries in the world to serve the European ports of Rotterdam and Zeebrugge.

The city was notorious for evading custom duties. Until the 18th century, all shipping arriving in Hull unloaded their wares at private staithes, or landing stages, adjoining the warehouses on the west bank of the Old Harbour of the River Hull. Smaller transit vessels, or lighters, were also used to transfer goods to and from larger vessels, which led to ample opportunity for goods to go astray amongst the many narrow streets and staithes. The huge trade of the port was causing concern to the customs and excise, who had no provision for a legal quay where goods could be appraised (Hull had been peculiarly exempt for hundreds of years, owing to the topography of the town which left no space along its river bank or wharves for a legal quay). The Dock Act of 1774 was to change all this with the creation of the Hull Dock Company, the first statutory dock company in Britain. In 1778 a new dock of 10 acres, then the largest inland dock in the country, was opened at right angles to, and entered from, the River Hull. Originally known as the Dock until the creation of the Humber Dock in 1809, it subsequently became the Old Dock. It was finally called Queen's Dock following a visit by Queen Victoria in 1854 when she sailed through the whole line of docks from the River Hull to the River Humber.

THE WATERFRONT & THE DOCKS

Above: QUEEN'S GARDENS c1965 H133114

Right: QUEEN'S GARDENS c1965 H133113

Ironically, having had no customs and excise provision during the 18th century, the north side of the dock was to become the site of Portcullis House, the local headquarters of Her Majesty's Customs and Excise. The building has been demolished and redeveloped as Queens Court, containing 115 luxury apartments and the new home of the BBC studios for East Yorkshire Humberside.

Far Right: THE WILBERFORCE MONUMENT c1955 H133001

THE WATERFRONT & THE DOCKS

THE DOCK OFFICES C1960 H133064

Queen's Gardens are complete with a large ornamental fountain, which stands in front of the former stable block of the North Eastern Railway Company.

The Old Dock was originally served by a small dock office near to its lock gates. It soon proved inadequate, and new offices were built at the north end of the High Street in 1820. These too soon proved to be insufficient to cope with the increase in trade caused by the construction of three more town docks, and were extended in 1840. Then the new offices at the west end of Queen's Dock

were built between 1867-71 to replace them. The dock closed in 1930, and following reclamation the site was redeveloped as the municipal Queen's Gardens (see H133002, page 59, and H133064).

The gardens remain a magnet for the inhabitants and visitors to this day. The many old buildings that still flank the sides of the gardens following the closure of the dock

THE WATERFRONT & THE DOCKS

betray the site of the former dock. The west end of the dock escaped the devastation of the surrounding area during the Second World War, and old drinking houses such as the Theatre Tavern and the Rugby Hotel (H133026, pages 60-61, centre left) survived to serve the small businesses that took over the former dockside buildings.

The east end of Queen's Gardens became the site of the Wilberforce Monument (H133001, page 63) when it was moved in 1935 from its original position on the Monument Bridge. A popular misconception, widely held in the city, is that the statue has moved several times during its lifetime. In reality it moved only once, in 1935, owing to traffic congestion; it was dismantled and re-erected on the site it still occupies.

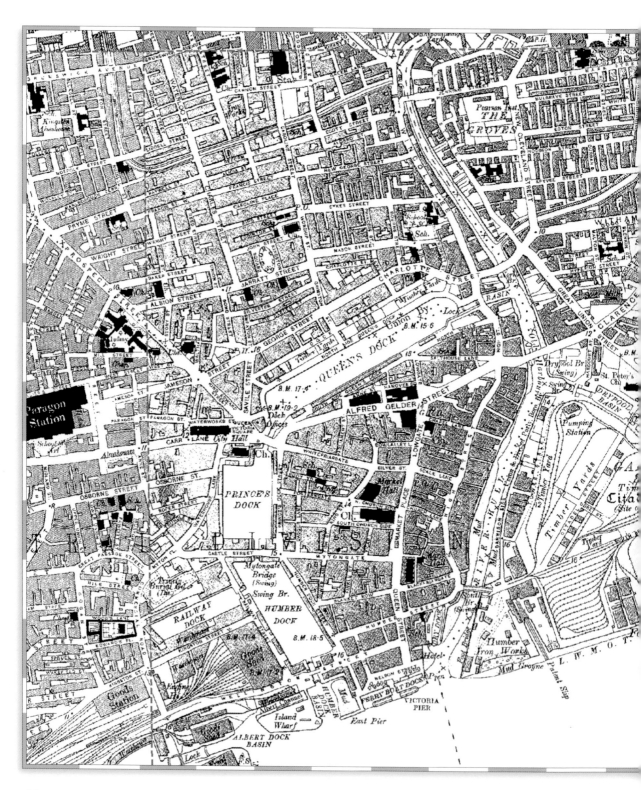

KINGSTON UPON HULL

AN ORDNANCE SURVEY MAP SHOWING KINGSTON-UPON-HULL
AND SURROUNDING AREAS c1900

EDUCATION, SCHOOLING & RELIGION

THE AREA around the gardens created from Queen's Dock and the devastation following the Second World War left large open spaces for new building projects. Among these were a new police headquarters, which was erected on the north side of the dock in 1959, and a technical college (H133110, pages 72-73) at the east end in 1962.

In 1887 Dr John Hymers, Rector of Brandesburton, bequeathed £170,000 to the Hull Corporation 'to found and endow' a grammar school. Unfortunately, his will was contested by his 80-year-old brother, Robert Hymers of Stokesley, who agreed in 1889 to give £50,000 to fulfil his brother's wishes. The newly-endowed school, designed by John Bilson (see 49834, page 71), was erected on the second site of the town's former Botanic Gardens.

The grammar schools of Hull could trace their origins back to the 14th century, but it was not until the 1950s that the city achieved full university status. At that time the University College, founded in 1925 with a gift of £250,000 from local businessman and philanthropist T R Ferens (see H133123), became a University in its own right.

Hull University has been gradually enlarged; modern buildings such as the physics lecture theatre and the Loten Hall of residence have been built (H133133, page 70), and the university has expanded to become one of the foremost universities in the north of England. The university campus contains

Education, Schooling & Religion

EDUCATION, SCHOOLING & RELIGION

the impressive Brynmor Jones Library, the domain of the novelist and poet Philip Larkin, who was chief librarian from 1955 until his death in 1985.

The city of Hull was never blessed with a cathedral or minster church like nearby York and Beverley; but it did have, according to Nikolaus Pevsner (in 'The Buildings of England: Yorkshire, York and the East Riding'), the largest parish church in area in England. The Church of the Holy and Undivided Trinity (49827, 49829 and 49830, pages 74-75) was originally constructed as a chapel of ease in circa 1285, possibly on the site of an earlier chapel. The

building is 285ft long, and the crossing tower is 150ft high. It did not become a parish church in its own right until 1661. The transepts and lower stages of the crossing tower contain some of the largest and earliest use of medieval brickwork in England.

Major restoration work of Holy Trinity Church was carried out internally between 1841 and 1845 under the supervision of the architect Henry Francis Lockwood. The nave was cleared of its galleries, and new pews to the designs of George Peck were fitted, along with a new pulpit of magnesian limestone. The exterior was restored

Education, Schooling & Religion

between 1859-72 by Sir George Gilbert Scott and again in 1906 by F S Brodrick. The church plate includes a cup dated 1587, the earliest example of a piece of silver bearing the Hull assay mark.

The large and rapid expansion into the suburbs during the late Georgian and Victorian periods resulted in the construction of some fine churches. The Anlaby Road, which ran west to the village of Anlaby alongside the Church of St Matthew (49832, page 74), was the first of Hull's main thoroughfares to be electrified for the introduction of the new tramway system of 1899. Many of Hull's Victorian churches disappeared with the creation of new housing estates following the slum clearances of the 1930s and 1950s. Modern churches include St Martin's Church, Anlaby Road (H133080, page 76), consecrated in 1939; it contains the 13th-century font from the ruined church of Nunkeeling.

The Spring Bank West housing estates, which had sprung up to the west of the city (H133075, page 77), were constructed with all the modern requisites for a healthier environment: wide open thoroughfares, houses with gardens, and small compact shopping areas complete with a small supermarket, a local pub and a cinema.

HYMERS COLLEGE 1903 49834

Opened in 1893, the school has gone from strength to strength; today it is one of the city's foremost educational establishments.

EDUCATION, SCHOOLING & RELIGION

THE TECHNICAL COLLEGE C1965 H133110

Above the site of the former lock gates of the old dock was built the superb nine-story
Technical College, designed by Frederick Gibberd and opened in 1962.

Education, Schooling & Religion

*Erected in 1870 at a cost of
£7,000 to the designs of Adams
& Kelly, St Matthew's Church
remains a prominent landmark
for the surrounding area; it is
the only surviving Victorian
church in Hull with a spire,
and is described by Pevsner as
the most impressive Victorian
church in this part of the city.*

Education, Schooling & Religion

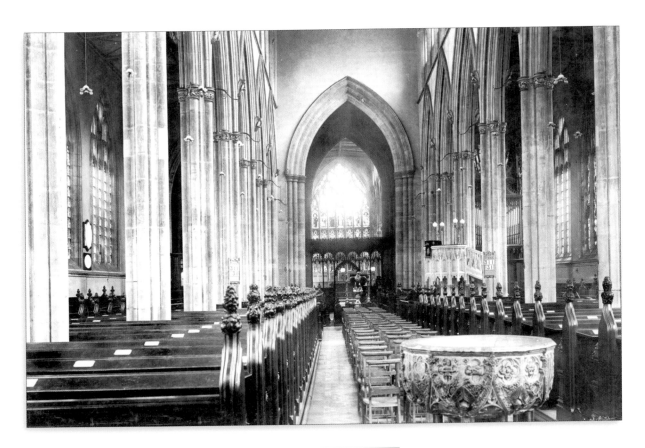

Above: Holy Trinity Church,
The Interior 1903 49830

Left: Holy Trinity Church,
The Interior 1903 49829

The church dominates the Market Place area. It is remarkably light and airy, despite being surrounded by buildings on all sides; the interior is well lit by some fine windows containing fragments of 15th- and 16th-century glass. There is a large painting of the Last Supper by James Parmentier (1711), and the aisles and south choir contain examples of medieval tombs, including those of the De La Pole family.

Above: St Martin's Church, Anlaby Road c1960 H133080

Left: Derringham Bank Methodist Church c1965 H133165

Derringham Bank Methodist Church, Spring Bank West, also of 1957-8, ministered to the inhabitants of the Derringham Bank, Calvert Road and Spring Bank West housing estates.

Education, Schooling & Religion

Below: The Church of the Ascension, Spring Bank West c1960 H133086

Originally intended as a parish hall, the Church of the Ascension was enlarged when a chancel was added in 1957-8 by F F Johnson; the former hall became the nave. The building was consecrated in 1958.

PARKS & LEISURE

THROUGHOUT the 19th century, the local Board of Health was constantly under pressure from reformers and pestered with demands for a public park. The reformers were finally listened to in 1860, when a committee was established to consider the practicability of providing a People's Park. After advertising for donations of land, the then Mayor, Zachariah Pearson, a local businessman and wealthy ship owner, offered 27 acres of land on the west side of the Beverley Road (see H133032, page 81). The layout and planting of the park was carried out to the designs of James Niven, the curator of the Botanic Gardens; the tree-lined avenues, containing gas-lighted roadways, led to the ten acres of land that Pearson, always a shrewd businessman, had reserved for the construction of large middle-class villas on the north, east and south sides of the park. The park contains fragments of the Old Town Hall which was demolished in 1912, and many Grade II listed buildings and statues.

West Park's entrance gates once contained a small branch library (H133154, page 85), designed by the city architect Joseph Hirst and Grade II listed, erected in 1905 with money donated by Andrew Carnegie. It is now sadly closed and awaiting an uncertain future.

In 1887 the East Park (49837A, H133029, page 84) became the third of the city's municipal parks; it was opened on the

WEST PARK 1903 49836

West Park was the second of Hull's municipal parks. It opened on a 31-acre site in 1885, and was noted for its fine open avenues of mature trees, its elaborate floral decorations, lakes and bandstand.

PARKS & LEISURE

The Lake, West Park c1955 H133021

Holderness Road on a 42-acre site. The park was famous for its rock gardens, through which ran the unofficial playground known as 'the Khyber Pass'. Its walls contained archaeological features such as a Roman mosaic and a bartizan (a corbelled corner turret) from the south-west bastion of the citadel of Henry VIII, which was demolished during the 19th century.

A pond in the park had been used, unofficially, for open air swimming by the boys since the early 1900s, and a second pond was in use by girls in the 1920s. By the end of the 1940s both had fallen into dilapidation; they were replaced in 1964 by a modern and very popular lido (see H133105, pages 84-85). The city is fortunate in being blessed with some fine gardens and parks in its town centre and suburbs.

Whilst not strictly a public park, Boothferry Park (H133153, page 85), became the second home of the town's football team, Hull City, visited by thousands of people at every home game during the football season. The football club was originally based on a site on the north side of the Anlaby Road near St Matthew's Church; it moved to its new ground on the Boothferry Road in 1947, and has now moved to a brand new state of the art stadium near to its original site on the Anlaby Road.

WEST PARK C1955 H133025

PEARSON PARK C1955 H133032

Parks & Leisure

East Park, The Boating Lake c1965 H133103

The size of East Park was greatly increased in 1913 when Hull's great benefactor Thomas Robinson Ferens gave a large parcel of land adjoining the park for the creation of a boating lake.

PARKS & LEISURE

Above: EAST PARK C1955 H133029

Below: EAST PARK 1903 49837A

Above: EAST PARK, THE LIDO c1965 H133105

Left Centre: THE FORMER CARNEGIE PUBLIC LIBRARY c1965 H133154

Left: HULL CITY FOOTBALL GROUND c1965 H133153

Names of Subscribers

The following people have kindly supported this book by purchasing limited
edition copies prior to publication.

The Baker Family, Belvoir Street, Hull
John Beecroft, Willerby. Happy Father's Day
George William Beilsten
Roy Berridge, Bilton
In loving memory of Rennard Allan Bexley
In memory of Edith Blakeston
John Bowes
To John L Bratton on his birthday
Mr & Mrs Ron Brignell
To Stephen Brint on your 80th Birthday
To Alan Brookes, in memory of our parents
As a tribute to my husband, Ken Broome
Mr N and Mrs A Brown and son Jason, Bilton
Mrs M O Brown, in memory of C W Brown
Brian & Marrie Buck, Married 1958
Dennis and Mona Burton, Hull
Alan and Sheila Button, May 2006
Ian Carmichael
The Carter Family, Bean Street
In loving memory of Miriam Currie, Hull
To Dad, happy 65th birthday, love Tracey and family
To Dawn and Debbie at Christmas, all my love, Dad
Herbert Dempsey
In memory of Harold Dixon, Hull
With love Dad, from The Dixons, 2006
To my daughter, Angela Dodson Smith
Clarence Draper, Hull, East Yorkshire
David Anthony Drury, Kingston-upon-Hull
Mrs Sharon Elbourne, Hull
Trevor Fields, 2006, Kingston-upon-Hull
To the Foster Family, Bilton, from Mam & Dad
In loving memory of George Dennis Garner
Happy Birthday Gary, from Mum & Dad
Margaret Elizabeth Gibson
Roger Golden
Ken & Beth Gray, Garden Village, Hull
Chris Hague, from Eileen
The Harrison Family, Kingston-upon-Hull
To lovely Mum and Gran, Elsie Haworth
Philip John Hirons, Hull City AFC Tigers
The Hodgins Family, Hull, East Yorks
For my son, Chistopher Irish, PI
The Jackson Family, Hull
Marjorie and Frank Jackson
Harry R Jackson, our beautiful son
The Jones Family of Kingston-upon-Hull
Mr & Mrs Jones, 50 Years of Marriage, 1956 - 2006
To Josh, Isobelle. Great Grandpop Frank
The Kavanaghs of Hull
In appreciation to Colin and Chris Larter
Kay Lashley
Val and Trevor Last of the Greenbury Family
The Leslie Family, Kingston-upon-Hull
William and Katharin Lillford
Family of Raymond & Beryl Linley, East Hull
To Bill Longbone on his 58th birthday

Tony Mackman
To Paul Makin & son Archie, luv Aunty Mo
Darren S J Marshall and family, Hull
Robert, Nicola and Sophie Mason, Hull
Mr Dennis Maynard, 130 Estcourt Street
The Mechen Family, Hull
For our son, Paul Antony Morfitt
To Mr & Mrs Murray, from Michelle & Scott
Fred Newmarch. Happy Birthday Dad, love Deb x
In memory of Kenneth E Nixon, Hull
To Richard North on his 50th Birthday
Mr Ian Pearce
To Stephen Petruniak, from his parents
Jim Portz, sailed from Hull, England, on MV 'Riley', 1954
John & Susan Power, Hull
Lavinia Priestley
The Prince Family, Hull
Jean Prosser
Mr J R Proudley on his birthday
Noel Rackley
To Rene at Christmas, with love from Len
To Douglas Rhodes, my precious Grandad
Tony Rippon
The Keith Roberts Family, Hull
To Robin, from your Yorkie tykes
Mr & Mrs P Robinson, Etherington Road, Hull
Eileen Robson, Hull
Mr & Mrs S Roughton, 34th anniversary
To George Rushworth, Hull, on his birthday
Mr and Mrs C Scorah, Hull
Malcolm Scott
Mr & Mrs Charles Scottow, 2006, Ruby Wedding
With love to Chris and Cliff Simister
To Joyce Simmond on her birthday
Olive & Arthur Smith, daughters Shirl & Lynne
Michael David Southcoat
As a tribute to H E and H M Spragg, Hull
Happy 80th Grandad, Harry Stephenson
In loving memory of our parents; Joan and Les Hawkes,
    and Agnes and Fred Stocks
David Sussams, Hull, North Humberside
Mr & Mrs W R Thomas, Hull
In memory of Timmy, our beloved dog
Ron Turner
Rose Turner
Richard A Usher, born 1972, Hull
A Alan Usher, Kingston-upon-Hull
To Phil Walker, luv Aunty Mo & Uncle Keith
Pat and Barrie Wardrobe
For Stanley and Edith Mary Watson
In memory of my Dad, John Ernest Watts
Kenneth Wiseman with my love, Judy
In loving memory of Dorothy Woods, Hull
To my mother, Lilian Wroeclough, Hull
To Zoe at Christmas, with love from Dad

INDEX

The Francis Frith Collection Titles

www.francisfrith.com

The Francis Frith Collection publishes over 100 new titles each year. A selection of those currently available is listed below. For latest catalogue please contact The Francis Frith Collection. **Town Books** 96 pages, approximately 75 photos. **County and Themed Books** 128 pages, approximately 135 photos (unless specified). Pocket Albums are miniature editions of Frith local history books 128 pages, approximately 95 photos.

Accrington Old and New
Alderley Edge and Wilmslow
Amersham, Chesham and Rickmansworth
Andover
Around Abergavenny
Around Alton
Aylesbury
Barnstaple
Bedford
Bedfordshire
Berkshire Living Memories
Berkshire Pocket Album
Blackpool Pocket Album
Bognor Regis
Bournemouth
Bradford
Bridgend
Bridport
Brighton and Hove
Bristol
Buckinghamshire
Calne Living Memories
Camberley Pocket Album
Canterbury Cathedral
Cardiff Old and New
Chatham and the Medway Towns
Chelmsford
Chepstow Then and Now
Cheshire
Cheshire Living Memories
Chester
Chesterfield
Chigwell
Christchurch
Churches of East Cornwall
Clevedon
Clitheroe
Corby Living Memories
Cornish Coast
Cornwall Living Memories
Cotswold Living Memories
Cotswold Pocket Album
Coulsdon, Chipstead and Woodmanstern
County Durham
Cromer, Sheringham and Holt
Dartmoor Pocket Album
Derby
Derbyshire
Derbyshire Living Memories
Devon
Devon Churches
Dorchester

Dorset Coast Pocket Album
Dorset Living Memories
Dorset Villages
Down the Dart
Down the Severn
Down the Thames
Dunmow, Thaxted and Finchingfield
Durham
East Anglia Pocket Album
East Devon
East Grinstead
Edinburgh
Ely and The Fens
Essex Pocket Album
Essex Second Selection
Essex: The London Boroughs
Exeter
Exmoor
Falmouth
Farnborough, Fleet and Aldershot
Folkestone
Frome
Furness and Cartmel Peninsulas
Glamorgan
Glasgow
Glastonbury
Gloucester
Gloucestershire
Greater Manchester
Guildford
Hailsham
Hampshire
Harrogate
Hastings and Bexhill
Haywards Heath Living Memories
Heads of the Valleys
Heart of Lancashire Pocket Album
Helston
Herefordshire
Horsham
Humberside Pocket Album
Huntingdon, St Neots and St Ives
Hythe, Romney Marsh and Ashford
Ilfracombe
Ipswich Pocket Album
Isle of Wight
Isle of Wight Living Memories
King's Lynn
Kingston upon Thames
Lake District Pocket Album
Lancashire Living Memories
Lancashire Villages

Available from your local bookshop or from the publisher

The Francis Frith Collection Titles (continued)

Lancaster, Morecambe and Heysham Pocket Album
Leeds Pocket Album
Leicester
Leicestershire
Lincolnshire Living Memoires
Lincolnshire Pocket Album
Liverpool and Merseyside
London Pocket Album
Ludlow
Maidenhead
Maidstone
Malmesbury
Manchester Pocket Album
Marlborough
Matlock
Merseyside Living Memories
Nantwich and Crewe
New Forest
Newbury Living Memories
Newquay to St Ives
North Devon Living Memories
North London
North Wales
North Yorkshire
Northamptonshire
Northumberland
Northwich
Nottingham
Nottinghamshire Pocket Album
Oakham
Odiham Then and Now
Oxford Pocket Album
Oxfordshire
Padstow
Pembrokeshire
Penzance
Petersfield Then and Now
Plymouth
Poole and Sandbanks
Preston Pocket Album
Ramsgate Old and New
Reading Pocket Album
Redditch Living Memories
Redhill to Reigate
Richmond
Ringwood
Rochdale
Romford Pocket Album
Salisbury Pocket Album
Scotland
Scottish Castles
Sevenoaks and Tonbridge
Sheffield and South Yorkshire Pocket Album
Shropshire
Somerset
South Devon Coast
South Devon Living Memories
South East London
Southampton Pocket Album
Southend Pocket Album
Southport

Southwold to Aldeburgh
Stourbridge Living Memories
Stratford upon Avon
Stroud
Suffolk
Suffolk Pocket Album
Surrey Living Memories
Sussex
Sutton
Swanage and Purbeck
Swansea Pocket Album
Swindon Living Memories
Taunton
Teignmouth
Tenby and Saundersfoot
Tiverton
Torbay
Truro
Uppingham
Villages of Kent
Villages of Surrey
Villages of Sussex Pocket Album
Wakefield and the Five Towns Living Memories
Warrington
Warwick
Warwickshire Pocket Album
Wellingborough Living Memories
Wells
Welsh Castles
West Midlands Pocket Album
West Wiltshire Towns
West Yorkshire
Weston-super-Mare
Weymouth
Widnes and Runcorn
Wiltshire Churches
Wiltshire Living Memories
Wiltshire Pocket Album
Wimborne
Winchester Pocket Album
Windermere
Windsor
Wirral
Wokingham and Bracknell
Woodbridge
Worcester
Worcestershire
Worcestershire Living Memories
Wyre Forest
York Pocket Album
Yorkshire
Yorkshire Coastal Memories
Yorkshire Dales
Yorkshire Revisited

See Frith books on the internet at www.francisfrith.com

FRITH PRODUCTS & SERVICES

Francis Frith would doubtless be pleased to know that the pioneering publishing venture he started in 1860 still continues today. Over a hundred and forty years later, The Francis Frith Collection continues in the same innovative tradition and is now one of the foremost publishers of vintage photographs in the world. Some of the current activities include:

Interior Decoration

Today Frith's photographs can be seen framed and as giant wall murals in thousands of pubs, restaurants, hotels, banks, retail stores and other public buildings throughout the country. In every case they enhance the unique local atmosphere of the places they depict and provide reminders of gentler days in an increasingly busy and frenetic world.

Product Promotions

Frith products are used by many major companies to promote the sales of their own products or to reinforce their own history and heritage. Frith promotions have been used by Hovis bread, Courage beers, Scots Porage Oats, Colman's mustard, Cadbury's foods, Mellow Birds coffee, Dunhill pipe tobacco, Guinness, and Bulmer's Cider.

Genealogy and Family History

As the interest in family history and roots grows world-wide, more and more people are turning to Frith's photographs of Great Britain for images of the towns, villages and streets where their ancestors lived; and, of course, photographs of the churches and chapels where their ancestors were christened, married and buried are an essential part of every genealogy tree and family album.

Frith Products

All Frith photographs are available Framed or just as Mounted Prints and Posters (size 23 x 16 inches). These may be ordered from the address below. From time to time other products - Address Books, Calendars, Table Mats, etc - are available.

The Internet

Already ninety thousand Frith photographs can be viewed and purchased on the internet through the Frith websites and a myriad of partner sites.

For more detailed information on Frith companies and products, look at this site:

www.francisfrith.com

See the complete list of Frith Books at:
www.francisfrith.com
This web site is regularly updated with the latest list of publications from The Francis Frith Collection. If you wish to buy books relating to another part of the country that your local bookshop does not stock, you may purchase on-line.

For further information, trade, or author enquiries please contact us at the address below:
The Francis Frith Collection, Frith's Barn, Teffont, Salisbury, Wiltshire, England SP3 5QP.
Tel: +44 (0) 1722 716 376 Fax: +44 (0) 1722 716 881   Email: sales@francisfrith.co.uk

See Frith books on the internet at www.francisfrith.com

FREE PRINT OF YOUR CHOICE

Mounted Print
Overall size 14 x 11 inches (355 x 280mm)

Choose any Frith photograph in this book.
Simply complete the Voucher opposite and return it with your remittance for £3.50 (to cover postage and handling) and we will print the photograph of your choice in SEPIA (size 11 x 8 inches) and supply it in a cream mount with a burgundy rule line (overall size 14 x 11 inches).
Please note: aerial photographs and photographs with a reference number starting with a "Z" are not Frith photographs and cannot be supplied under this offer. Offer valid for delivery to one UK address only.

PLUS: **Order additional Mounted Prints at HALF PRICE - £9.50 each** (normally £19.00)
If you would like to order more Frith prints from this book, possibly as gifts for friends and family, you can buy them at half price (with no additional postage and handling costs).

PLUS: **Have your Mounted Prints framed**
For an extra £18.00 per print you can have your mounted print(s) framed in an elegant polished wood and gilt moulding, overall size 16 x 13 inches (no additional postage and handling required).

IMPORTANT!

These special prices are only available if you use this form to order. You must use the ORIGINAL VOUCHER on this page (no copies permitted). We can only despatch to one UK address. This offer cannot be combined with any other offer.

Send completed Voucher form to:
The Francis Frith Collection, Frith's Barn, Teffont, Salisbury, Wiltshire SP3 5QP

CHOOSE A PHOTOGRAPH FROM THIS BOOK

Voucher for **FREE** and *Reduced Price Frith Prints*

Please do not photocopy this voucher. Only the original is valid, so please fill it in, cut it out and return it to us with your order.

Picture ref no	Page no	Qty	Mounted @ £9.50	Framed + £18.00	Total Cost £
		1	Free of charge*	£	£
			£9.50	£	£
			£9.50	£	£
			£9.50	£	£
			£9.50	£	£
			£9.50	£	£

Please allow 28 days for delivery.
Offer available to one UK address only

* Post & handling	£3.50
Total Order Cost	£

Title of this book . . . .

I enclose a cheque/postal order for £ . . . . made payable to 'The Francis Frith Collection'

OR please debit my Mastercard / Visa / Maestro card, details below

Card Number

Issue No (Maestro only)   Valid from (Maestro)

Expires   Signature

Name Mr/Mrs/Ms . . . .

Address . . . .

. . . .

. . . .

. . . . Postcode . . . .

Daytime Tel No . . . .

Email . . . .

Valid to 31/12/12

Free Print – see overleaf

Can you help us with information about any of the Frith photographs in this book?

We are gradually compiling an historical record for each of the photographs in the Frith archive. It is always fascinating to find out the names of the people shown in the pictures, as well as insights into the shops, buildings and other features depicted.

If you recognize anyone in the photographs in this book, or if you have information not already included in the author's caption, do let us know. We would love to hear from you, and will try to publish it in future books or articles.

Our production team

Frith books are produced by a small dedicated team at offices in the converted Grade II listed 18th-century barn at Teffont near Salisbury, illustrated above. Most have worked with The Francis Frith Collection for many years. All have in common one quality: they have a passion for The Francis Frith Collection. The team is constantly expanding, but currently includes:

Andrew Alsop, Paul Baron, Jason Buck, John Buck, Jenny Coles, Heather Crisp, David Davies, Natalie Davis, Louis du Mont, Isobel Hall, Chris Hardwick, Julian Hight, Peter Horne, James Kinnear, Karen Kinnear, Tina Leary, Stuart Login, Sue Molloy, Sarah Roberts, Kate Rotondetto, Eliza Sackett, Terence Sackett, Sandra Sampson, Adrian Sanders, Sandra Sanger, Julia Skinner, Lewis Taylor, Will Tunnicliffe, David Turner and Ricky Williams.